Gaining the competitive edge in life & business

Martin B. Ayles

Published by Brolga Publishing Pty Ltd
PO Box 12544 A'Beckett St Melbourne Australia 8006
ABN 46 063 962 443
email: sales@brolgapublishing.com.au
web: www.brolgapublishing.com.au

Copyright © 2012 Martin B. Ayles
First printed in 2003

   Gaining the competitive edge in life & business
   Martin B. Ayles
   ISBN 9781922036667

National Library of Australia Cataloguing-in-Publication entry
Printed in Adelaide
Cover design by David Khan
Typesetting by Wanissa Somsuphangsri & Wendy Aird

Gaining the competitive edge in life & business

A reality check
to really get your
life moving!

Martin B. Ayles

Contents

Foreword

I first met Martin in a café at 10 o'clock one night. I was on my way home from work in the cold and rain and remember thinking that all I wanted to do was go to bed. At the time I was cold, confused and depressed! I was renting a nice little house, had lots of toys that I had bought with my credit cards, and a car that I owed about $10,000 more on than what it was worth!

I was on what I thought was a good income, but most of it was going to pay for my debt and the lifestyle I thought I should have. At the end of the day, I had very little money for someone in my position.

At that stage, I was employed as an investment consultant for a major bank. Imagine how I felt each day, knowing that I was financially going backward but still having to sell myself to clients as a savvy investment advisor – just so they would buy an investment that may return a measly 5%! Something needed to change and it had to begin with 'the man in the mirror'!

Martin contacted me through a mutual friend and suggested we should have a chat. That chat would become a life-changing event. What we discussed over the next few hours was a world that I thought was not achievable by someone like myself – a world that only the lucky or the rich played in. We talked about things such as the difference between good and bad debt, positive cash flow, generating income from the market with limited risk, and most importantly, how to make a greater contribution to family and friends.

Martin showed me not only how I could rescue myself from the mound of consumer debt I had created, but also how I could build an amount of wealth that hours before I thought was inconceivable.

The best part of Martin's plan was that most of this could happen with less exertion from myself than most people put into their jobs! The key was my commitment to myself that I needed to change before anything else would. Then the world would be mine for the taking!

In the 18-months since our meeting, and with a few simple lessons from Martin, I have compiled over $2.3 million dollars in assets which generates the passive cash flow which supports my living while also servicing the 'good' debt.

I no longer work for the bank! I had to quit because there were too many opportunities for making money that I was missing by being in an office Monday to Friday, 9-5! Working was costing me money! Imagine that – I could no longer afford to work!

In the time since our first chat, I have learned many more lessons, but only because Martin gave me the confidence to take on new ideas and new strategies, and taught me that it's OK to make mistakes along the way. I have made mistakes, as you will too, but most importantly I have only made them once!

The choice of freedom is a conscious one. I can choose to sit and watch TV or I can choose to read a book on how to buy property without any money! I can choose to eat poorly or I can choose to be fit and healthy. I have chosen to be wealthy. I am in control. It's my choice, not anyone else's.

I thank Martin for giving me the confidence to make those choices. I thank Martin for giving me the tools to make informed choices. I am now so scared of being 'normal' that it won't happen!

By letting Martin into your life you will gain control of your life too!

It's all up to you!

Ben Fitzsimons
Adelaide, South Australia.

Chapter 1

To begin with

Throughout this book you may find parts of it a little blunt. I guess you could call it brutally honest! Some of what I have written may offend. If it does, it may be because I am simply describing things that may have happened or be happening in your life; things that you may not have faced up to yet.

Please, do not take offence if something does hit a nerve or two, just take action and change instead!

You can choose not to read on if you do get offended, but it is not meant intentionally to upset you, so don't take it personally. Just take personal responsibility!

If this still scares you, then put this book down and quit reading. Just remember though, the challenge with society today is that quitting is the easy option and keep in mind no matter what you do in life, you can always quit! So don't quit. Step up and take the challenge! You owe it to yourself and maybe to others as well. By taking action from reading this book, it may help you to positively change and influence someone else's life for the better – and all from the knowledge you gained, simply because you chose to read this book to the end!

Although far from an easy challenge to solve, a change to the education system would be a great milestone in the future of generations to come. As to what these changes would have to be? Well that would be a very long chapter and depending on who has the input as to how many suggestions for changes to the education system there would need to be.

Our style of teaching is out dated and fairly mundane. I am sure that there is some passionate teachers out there but they now have to spend half their days worrying about running the metal detectors or abiding by the strict regulations of being able to apply disciplinary action to students.

Teaching out of text books is more or less a parrot fashion method of teaching and although needed in some areas, every person has a different method of absorbing information and the way in that they learn and perceive information.

Children are often not interested in some of the subjects that schools teach. If the teaching method were fun and lively, the students would retain more knowledge and enjoy attending school a lot more. Unfortunately, we teach through the memorization of textbooks, instead of learning through lessons. For example, if they used the concept of a board game, such as Monopoly as a teaching methodology for teaching life and investing skills, then I am certain that they would be pleasantly surprised at the results.

The first reason for this is that life and investing is a game. The second reason is that it is fun. It involves basic math, buying property, taking mortgages, obeying the law and avoiding jail, paying bills and fines, using leverage and collecting or paying rent. But most of all, the lesson is that four houses equals one hotel! You see, the lesson behind Monopoly is more than a game just about money. It is about starting off small with one house and collecting a little rent, then mortgaging for your second house and collecting more rent and so on, until once you have four houses that you can trade up to buy a hotel, because a hotel provides a lot more income than a house.

The lesson you get from monopoly is that the knowledge required to do the small property deal is the same as the big hotel deal, but if you didn't start with the small deal first then you cannot do the bigger hotel deals. Monopoly also teaches patience and the value of time.

I guess the sad part about society today is that computer games have taken over games like Monopoly, and these days a lot of kids are often playing violent games rather than real life games. You see, games allow you to be creative without any real risk. They allow the imagination to run free, and today when negative games with poor or no lessons are being drummed into kids, one must assume that these games will have some influence on the child as they grow up.

So I hope that my influence will help to educate and assist children and their parents as well. I promise to donate a lot of my time to fun useful education for the future and one day I may even be able to convince someone to make positive changes to the education system.

At the age of 27, I consider myself young. I have had nearly ten years of full-time work experience, as well as various attempts at my own businesses and studying as well. In that time, I have also been unemployed and in a lot of consumer debt. I've had everything from credit cards to store accounts and when the banks started chasing me I was continually borrowing money from anyone or anything to pay that money back. It was a vicious cycle.

I was fortunate to be introduced to network marketing at just 17 years old. One of the greatest benefits I had from being involved in this business was a program for the business builders that involved a book of the month and an audiotape of the week. I always read the books and listened to the tapes over and over, and found myself enjoying them and looking forward to all the new ones. I know to this day that if it wasn't for the books and tapes I would most probably be in some undesirable situation somewhere.

The education process offered was interesting. They had seminars with great guest speakers like Laurie Lawrence and Peter Daniels. I learned great lessons from being involved with network marketing.

A friend from the network marketing business realized I had a genuine interest in improving my financial position. He invited me to a 3-hour seminar. I was so intrigued by the presentation that I went back the next night! On offer was a one-day workshop on real estate investing with expert Dolf de Roos. I had to put the $1,000 registration fee on my credit card, but for some reason I knew I needed to be there. That was in 1998 and I spent the next two years getting out of debt. At the time getting a job was the only way I knew how to get out of debt, so after 2 years of hard scrimping and saving, I was able to purchase my very first investment property in July of 2000!

And the rest as they say is history. In less than 2-years I have purchased over $5-million in holding property and made a lot of cash along the way. I have been able to generate more cash flow using the stock market and my real estate investments. My family and friends noticed a change as I went from unemployed to a wealth of information on investing and money. I even started assisting a lot of others to do the same as I was doing.

Friends began requesting help to change their financial position and their friends also came to me to find out what it was I had done to become wealthy at such a young age. It was then that I had to begin charging, as demand increased for my time and it got to a point where I was charging people a few thousand dollars to hang out with me, hear their challenges and help them deal with their financial issues. Usually when we got to the bottom of it there was a stack of emotional stuff jamming their brain, so they couldn't fill it with good data or the information they needed to make a stack of cash.

Their financial position when they came to me for help was often a very empty wallet with a full credit card or two hanging out of it with a 20% per annum interest charge attached. You see, it's often not simply bad money management (although that's a good starting point) it's the life management and your own mind management that makes a difference to the size of your wallet and bank account, not the cash! Cash is just the physical result of doing enough of the right things for yourself and others. There is more detail coming on this so hang in there.

After I put together some ideas on what I wanted to write about I came to the realisation that this book could assist anyone who is prepared to get off their butt and push themselves along.

The challenge I had was that I did not know what direction to take with my life after leaving school. I kept going to seminars and workshops, read books and listened to tapes. I was trying to find answers.

The simple fact is that the answer begins with you. Education begins when you leave school – it doesn't end.

Accept that you and I can always be better, and realize that success is whatever you choose it to be. The word success is a generalization and you should relate the meaning of it to the achievement of your own goals and desires, not someone else's.

Although some of my achievements were based around investment goals, it's not so much the money that drove me to go out and invest to become wealthy, but more so the pain of doing what I was doing, as a mundane employee day-in, day-out. I couldn't see the light at the end of the tunnel by selling my labour for $10-15/hour while knowing that there were only so many hours in a day. I realized that my earning potential was limited by how much of my time I could sell, so something had to change. I needed to invest and free up my time so I could follow my vision and become the best I could.

It is about becoming the person it takes to achieve what you set out to do, and the lessons you get along the way.

Success is a personal thing and should be based on what you want to do, not based on your friends or family's choices for you. They often have a different view of what you will or should become. Besides, is what they're doing what you want to become? If not, why take their advice? Sure, listen to their opinion but remember, it's exactly that – an opinion! It's your ship so take control and steer it yourself before they try and take over and ram it up the backend of someone else. Remember, I am just the compass giving you direction. Chances are you'll be off course more often than not, but you will end up at **your** destination eventually.

Having not completed school or tertiary education I have

this attitude that anyone can achieve what they want. I couldn't care less if you don't have a PhD or degree, or even if you didn't make it past the 9th grade. Personally, I cannot even do basic maths. I know how to add, subtract and divide using a calculator and it usually takes me a couple of goes to work out a percentage.

Another major influence on this book was that I had been working full-time for 10-years, and was heading in the same direction that a lot of society had chosen. I knew if I continued down the same path then life was not going to change until I chose to make the changes happen. Once I made those changes I found I had achieved more than most people twice my age! I realized then that we all have a choice – keep doing the same old thing year-in, year-out – or change!

I have found that if the mere thought of, or talking about goals and dreams were painful to anyone, they were probably the people whose car was rejected by a scrap metal yard, or whose communication was via an argument or who demonstrated a lack of ability to use their ears instead of their gob, or the ones who couldn't remember what state of the country their children lived in. It's pretty sad and no wonder they found goals hard to achieve. Remember, self-belief is the first thing any goal requires.

I don't care if you're single and young, middle-aged and married or divorced, widowed, or older and wiser. It really doesn't matter! By simply taking a few steps first in your mind, then in your physical life, things will change so rapidly that you'll be blown away. Remember this message:

Don't Quit!
If it's not working, change what you are doing!

There is a big difference between simply changing actions

to get to where you are trying to go, and quitting. Don't quit!

One thing I can promise you is that you will come across a time in your life when it is all going to blow up in your face. You will want to run - but don't be a handbag and run. Turn around and run head on into your challenge. We will work on this together later in this book, but I want you to step-up and accept the fact that you are going to face fears both physically and mentally. I identify when fear is controlling my state of mind by understanding that fear can subconsciously drive you in the direction of quitting. So, to me that is a simple way of identifying when fear is controlling my state of mind. I become aware of that fear and I tackle it straight away.

I have found that other people's words can create unnecessary fear to a large degree. I may discuss with them a big real estate deal I am about to do and they say things like, *"What if interest rates go up?"* or *"What if the market has a down turn?"* and I have just signed the contracts and I start to wonder that maybe I made the wrong decision! The simple way around this is not talk to them about it and only seek advice from someone who has done it! Keep in mind that 'FEAR' stands for: *'False Expectations Appearing Real.'*

So let's get on with it and I ask you to keep your sense of humour throughout this book and life. There is no monetary value on a good laugh and it's also good for you. What might seem bad in your life at the moment may be something you will be able to laugh about in years to come! We are all under the pressure of 'modern day' life, and seem to be busy doing more and more while achieving less and less. Peak hour traffic is getting worse and the work hours are getting longer. Holidays seem less frequent and shorter and we all feel like we are getting old too quickly.

This is not the way it's supposed to feel! Often times the only reason we are unhappy in life, I find, is because we are missing out on enjoying the pleasure of the important things that money doesn't buy. Things such as laughter, family involvement, giving and receiving love, and helping someone become something. But the reality is we live in a society that is dominated by money in the physical aspects of life. Simply put, if you have CASH it's a lot easier to live your life, fulfil your goals, and assist someone else to experience the things that money can't buy.

The point being, it is impossible to make it through the physical plane of life without CASH, and what you want will determine how much of it (cash) you need. So how much do you really need?

Making money is easy. It's about doing whatever it takes to become the person who is wealthy – that's what counts. I see it as being no different from a successful sports person. They work hard for a long time and often get no money, but they have a cabinet full of trophies instead. They have fans and they have critics. They train, practice and prepare harder every day. And they make sacrifices most people could never contemplate. Then one day a young Adelaide boy called Lleyton Hewitt wins the US open tennis tournament and Wimbledon, and takes home $1-2 million in prize money. Pretty cool yeah, but I promise you one thing, he's underpaid! If you had to go through the pain of what he did to get to where he's got, then you would also know that the money doesn't justify the sacrifices made. Besides, I'm sure Lleyton wouldn't have been doing it for the money in the first place. He just wanted it bad enough and understood that, 'winning isn't everything, but wanting to win is'.

I don't really need a lot of stuff in my life. Love, health and freedom of time are good enough for me. But hey, if you have to drive to your beach house in your Ferrari, then that can be fun too.

Now I know that I'm far from perfect. However, I feel that if I can change someone's life for the better by sharing the experiences that I've had in an easy-to-read format, with a bit of humour and reality, then it was worth my time to write this book. I've met so many great people in my life, because I've made it a priority to get around the best people in any area or field of life I'm interested in. I believe everybody has the ability to be and do something special with their life, but every now and then we just need someone else to believe in us.

It is difficult to keep on swimming against the current in life, trying to continually improve yourself and achieve the tasks or goals you set. There will always be setbacks and interruptions along the way that will slow you down, but as long as you keep your destination in mind and get back on track as soon as possible, then you will keep heading in the right direction.

This book is designed to give you a set of values and opinions to consider throughout your daily life. It will also make you aware of your daily actions and help you to take note of what you are doing with your time. As you come across situations, you may need to make a decision on the spot either way. This book will help you to assess your position in life and view your decision from all available points of view.

Whether it helps you make a positive change to your life financially, physically or emotionally, as long as it makes a difference, then I know I have made a contribution to the world, and I'll know it was worthwhile writing this book!

Chapter 2

Your Choice

You are where you are today as a result of your choices yesterday. You may believe that someone else is responsible for where you are at in life, but that is nothing more than passing the blame. The reality is that there is not a thing you can do about your past and no matter where you are presently in life, you can make changes to tomorrow's results, but it has to be your choice. What you get tomorrow is nothing more than the results of what you do today.

Let me explain.

Let's say you have a weight problem, that is not related to any medical condition apart from not getting off your butt and doing some exercise. One reason you may be overweight is that you shove too much fatty fried food in your mouth. People who are starving are not overweight, so isn't it obvious that one way we become overweight is by eating excessive, fatty food? Excess food and fat makes you fat!

That's my 'brief' perspective on dieting! In short that's not all you need to know about dieting, but the point I am making is that you're the one who chooses what goes into your mouth. Just because there are a lot of TV adverts saying its ok to eat their sugar-filled, colour-filled and additive-filled product, does not make it OK to eat. Is this a book about diet? No, it's a book about choices.

In your life so far, you have gotten exactly what you chose to get and it just seems that all too often people take the pie instead of the salad. All we need to do, is make a choice either way, but usually a whole stack of excuses and poor reasons get in the way of not choosing the better option for the long-term gain.

Then we end up with the pie, because we are all so busy and it's quick, easy and we can eat it on the run. We are all so busy and even though a lot of us are suffering either financially or emotionally as a result of being busy, it seems we try to bury the pain of our present situation by consuming a pie loaded with 30 grams of fat disguised with ketchup! We know it will hurt us later one way or another. The result is a yummy and short-lived nice feeling as we gobble down the pie. For a brief moment in life, we can enjoy the so-called meaning of feeling good. About 15-minutes later when our body is trying desperately to absorb the greasy pastry, salt, sugar and butter from the pie we begin to realise that maybe it wasn't the right thing to do.

Then we compensate by saying, *"That's OK, I'll start eating well tomorrow,"* but as we both know, for most of us tomorrow never seems to come. And then along comes the weekend so we justify the junk food intake again by saying, *"That's OK, I'll start eating well Monday,"* then off we go again on our excuse-making journey never seeming to make any changes to our habits!

One of the best things I ever learned from Australian Entrepreneur, Brad Sugars, was that in life there is a line and we can play above it or below it, but ultimately it's your choice where you play.

It goes like this:

Accountability
Responsibility
Ownership

_____

Blame
Denial
Excuses

So what side of the line are you going to choose to live from now on? These days a lot of people in society are living below the line and this is one of the reasons why we have so many legal cases going on. Everyone wants to sue someone because it was someone else's fault. It's also happening in relationships and businesses. Liability cases are more common than ever. So if your job sucks, your boss is a jerk and your bank balance is continually heading in the minus direction, then ask yourself a few questions ...

Do you choose to work there?

Do you choose to accept the hourly pay rate you're on?

Did you decide to buy some stuff on credit card that you could have done without?

It's not anyone's fault but your own, as to where you are in life ... In some way we've all been through tough situations in life, granted some are worse than others, but if you're reading this and saying _"Oh yeah, but what about me, I had a rough upbringing,"_ or _"My family never had any money and I didn't get the same opportunities as others,"_ then you are living in the state of **blame** which is below the line. You can't change the past so get over it quickly and move forward. Looking back and feeling sorry for yourself is just going to delay the desired outcome that you deserve.

You choose which side of the line you want to live on. You

can make **excuses** like, *"I don't earn enough money and that's the reason I am broke,"* or you can just **deny** being in a situation full stop. *"Wasn't me!"* is a common one for this. The reality is you get exactly what you ask for in life, whether it is your financial position, your health or your chosen career path. No matter what it is you're doing, you will have to choose what side of the line you live on from now on.

So now, if you weren't already, I hope you've decided to live above the line! I found that when I learnt this concept everything I achieved in life seemed to come back to what side of the line I had chosen to live on. I have met rich people who are unhealthy and I have met healthy people who are poor, but what it came back to was that they had chosen to become rich and forgotten about health. The healthy person was poor because they had focused on health and fitness but not money and wealth.

The reality is in some areas of their lives they had chosen to live above the line and in other areas of life they had chosen to live below the line. So my question to you is this … What areas of your life do you believe you need to change to play above the line? It may be your physical fitness, financial position, relationship, your job, or your personal development and the list goes on.

Just by moving above the line won't change anything; you are still going to have to do some work when you get there. But until you decide to go, there is no point trying to fix anything. Self-doubt and laziness are the two main reasons why you may have trouble getting started. So move your butt and make your decision quickly to change. The quicker you move above the line the quicker you can get through all the other stuff you have to do and get rich!

Chapter 3

Deferred Responsibility

As it says, deferring means to 'delay'. In life there could be many times where you choose to defer responsibility because of things like your comfort zone or fear. But, now you have chosen to live above the line and take responsibility for yourself, you need to ask yourself what it is in life you are deferring responsibility on. I've found that whenever I've been able to help someone to overcome the challenge of not deferring responsibility any longer, they seem to progress forward very fast!

Put simply the message is …

'DO NOT DEFER RESPONSIBILITY' any longer!

For example, if you're in a relationship and you think you don't want to be in it or you are unhappy, then rather than hanging out to see if it gets better with time or hoping things will change, understand that the situation won't change until you do. If you repeat the same actions and live each day the same way then how do you expect the relationship to improve?

Now I'm not saying that walking away from the relationship is the only way to fix it. You may accept responsibility by taking up relationship counselling or by reading a book on the subject of relationship issues. Or perhaps talking to a friend, who has been through a similar situation, may put some light on the subject.

At least when you face up to it and take action to change for the better, you can move on. And what was once a problem then becomes a challenge, because you choose to overcome it by accepting responsibility first, and then taking action to change the situation. I guarantee you will become a better person as a result of stepping up and facing your challenge head-on rather than continually deferring it.

Another example of deferring responsibility could be if you are behind in your loan payments. Rather than hiding, avoiding phone calls or debt collection letters, try what I have done in the past … pick up the phone and ring them. Introduce yourself and say, *"Hi, it's me calling."* Tell them your name and say, *"I'm the one who owes you fourteen thousand on credit, and haven't paid you for two months, but I'm calling to make payment arrangements with you!"* Simple isn't it!

Don't bother lying, it's too much hard work, because then you need to remember what you told them – and that takes up too much of the effort that you could be using to get rich. Just say …*"Hi, I'm broke and owe you fourteen grand."* Besides, they have the problem not you. They're the ones who are out of pocket the fourteen grand. So now that you faced up to it who has the problem!

Before you can get rich, you have to accept responsibility for the position you are in, and not defer it any longer. All deferring responsibility does is create clutter, both physical clutter and mental clutter.

The quicker you clean up and face your responsibilities, the quicker the clutter goes and you will progress forward much faster. So call up your creditors, but don't tell them too much detail about where you live (as they may come and try and sell your undies to St. Vinnies to recover the debt!) Just tell them the payment plan that you have worked out and how much money they will get. But whatever you do, stick to your word and make these payments, as your integrity may be all you have left. Once you shaft people by going against your word, it can be bloody hard to get anywhere in life!

Chapter 4

Physical Action

I still have fears and challenges like everyone. I deal with them firstly by standing up and choosing to accept them; secondly by accepting responsibility for where I'm at; and then thirdly by taking physical action to change the situation I'm in.

You can do the same thing! You have to face your fears and overcome these challenges that have bugged you for donkey's years, before you can move on to follow your true desires and dreams. But when you release all the handbrakes that slow you down, remember it was because you chose to let them slow you down, you can't blame them!

Once you have faced **all** the challenges you need to overcome, you must then take physical action to begin to overcome them. The answers you were missing will be in the result of the outcome. I'll use the relationship example again as divorce is so common these days.

For example:

By taking the physical action of walking to the cupboard, getting out the Yellow Pages, looking up the relationship counselling service and booking an appointment; then actually showing up, telling them nothing but the truth, and paying the bill in full as you leave, AND then putting into action what the counsellor recommended, you'll find the challenge will be solved, sooner or later, and most of the time with a positive outcome.

Now it may take four visits and six months to take shape, but just by trying the things recommended the results will soon show up, but only if you're true to yourself and give it a go.

By taking physical action, ringing up and making the appointment, you may have achieved nothing more than the understanding that by taking these physical steps, you'll get to the outcome eventually! Remember this – choices. It's all about the choices we make. Then accept the situation and take action to change, if need be. Once it is fixed then we can move on to our next challenge and start working on it straight away. Do not procrastinate in taking physical action to overcome challenges as this will stall your progress forward. Be aware that by stalling you can easily end up talking yourself back to living below the line, as this is where we are in our comfort zone.

I have friends who are trying to buy real estate at the same rate I do. But the point they miss is the degree of physical action that I apply. For example if I need to look at real estate, it means taking physical action and that could mean going out at ten or eleven in the evening and driving around the suburbs I'm interested in everyday for a month. But if that's what it takes to find one to buy, then so be it! I'm on the hunt, looking out for 'For Sale' signs, even ones with sold stickers on them. I use high beam on the car headlights and drive up the driveways and shine the lights on the house and check it out. No one in the houses ever seems to care, because they are always so glued to the TV watching some mindless junk, a few high beamers down the hallway won't budge them off their couch!

I have a notepad in the car and I write down the address of the properties, the agent and a brief description of the house and even the sold ones. Then the very next morning, I call the agents to discuss the properties in more detail, making sure I find out what the ones that were sold went for, as this helps me get to know the area better.

I then make appointments to go through and view the ones I decide to look at, and then within a week of looking, I will have made an offer on a property. Perhaps it's a run down house near to the beach, so I grab a paintbrush or two, throw up a fence and toss around some garden mulch and whammo! I pick up a cool fifty grand cash when some bloke rolls up to my auction and he and his wife get all emotional over the house and pay above full price for it!

At the end of the auction everyone is clapping, so he feels good. But are they clapping because they are impressed with him, or are they clapping thinking, *"Ha, ha, good one Wally – we can't believe you just paid so much for that house!"*

So where was he that night I was out looking at houses? If he wasn't watching TV that same night jammed into the corner of his financed couch after his day of eating pies and chips washed down with a whole load of "Diet Fizzy Drinks" (because he is watching his weight!) then maybe he could have been the one making the profit instead of me.

The only difference is I chose to take physical action to change my financial position and the outcome was another fifty grand towards my Ferrari! Not bad for a 27 year old who missed out on a bit of mindless TV!

Well that should have you thinking a bit differently about physical action and the results and outcome differences that taking action can provide. I think we have the ball rolling so let's keep on with it and move onto the best reality check of them all. That is, understanding the difference between sacrifice and discipline.

Chapter 5

Sacrifice and Discipline

For you to have read this book far, you have had to apply both sacrifice and discipline. You may have had to sacrifice some TV time and it has taken some discipline to keep reading. (Only 10% of books ever get read entirely.) Once a blinding flash of the obvious (BFO) made me realize that sacrifice and discipline go hand-in-hand with each other, I suddenly started getting amazingly great results in my life!

Recently I decided to lose weight, as I was heading in the cuddly direction. So I bought a book called 'Fit for Life' by Harvey and Marilyn Diamond and although it required a strong level of self-discipline, all I did was sacrifice junk foods. By doing this I ended up 7kgs lighter in about 5 weeks. I cut out the crap foods, ate primary produce (eg. no manufactured foods) and drank predominately water! I could still have a beer on the weekend if I wanted to and still not end up looking like a beached whale on my local beach!

It really is so simple yet it seems so stupid! But no one seems to be able to stick to something for more than two days when trying to get a result. We live in a microwave society where everyone wants to press a button and have the results in two minutes. Hence the reason that most achieve two days worth of results per year in their lives.

If you need to lose weight then you have to sacrifice pies for salads. Right? So, it must take a certain amount of discipline when you are standing at the takeaway counter not to order the pie and take the salad instead. Right? Well it makes sense to me!

So I don't get it? Why is every one eating the pies? It's because you link pleasure to eating the pie and pain to the salad. That's why. Perhaps the thoughts are, *"The pies are yummy! One won't hurt and I deserve it. I exercise so it's OK for me to have it!"* And so on. As for the salad, *"Well, it's a little bland. I feel like hot food today, and a salad won't fill me up. I need protein so I had better have the pie,"* and that's how you justify having the pie.

We all know what happens fifteen minutes later. I don't want to start on the topics of pain and pleasure, but I do recommend an Anthony Robbins seminar or his 30-day Personal Power Program. Alternatively, check out his website to discover more on this.

But I digress; I'm mean to simply point out the difference between sacrifice and discipline. If you need to go out and look at property then it takes discipline to get off your couch, take physical action and drive around the suburbs until you find your Ferrari deposits!

Then the sacrifice means missing out on TV. Don't let this worry you, just ask someone at work the next day or in the lunch shop as you order your salad, what it was you missed on TV the night before. They will sit down and tell you everything you missed on the idiot box as they're cramming a pie and a chocolate donut down their traps, as they only have a fifteen minute lunch break because they are too busy at work, making the owner of the company rich. And by the way, that owner is probably in Hawaii on his/her monthly golf trip!

If you want to get up and go to the gym in the morning

then you have to have the discipline to not bash the snooze button on your alarm clock and actually get out of bed. You will have to sacrifice some sleep, but the outcome will be that your fitness will improve by going to the gym. The thing is sacrifice must go hand-in-hand with discipline. They go hand-in-hand, because you can't have one without the other. When I see people around me who are not really achieving anything, except a pay cheque each week and ten hours sleep a night on a diet that wouldn't allow their body to be used for a science lab test while living in a financial position that keeps them 3 weeks from broke, then all I can do is relate it to a lack of self-sacrifice and discipline.

You see it takes sacrifice and discipline to make good choices, to live above the line and to take physical action. Nothing will be attracted to you until you choose to utilise self-sacrifice and discipline in your life, to get what you really want.

So next time you're lying on the couch chewing on the remote control, watching the Time Vanishing machine (that's what TV stands for) ask yourself this, *"Should I be giving myself a dose of self-discipline? And if so, what do I need to sacrifice at the moment?"* Then I can go on my merry way of achieving what I should be, rather than staying in zombie-mode glued to the idiot box.

Now don't get me wrong – it's going to hurt … with all sacrifice and discipline there is going to be pain. A lot of people know this, and it is sometimes easy to let the pain get the better of us and give up. There are, however, only two types of pain, the pain of discipline and the pain of regret!

Go on, get off your rear end and give it a go. I promise it won't kill you. As Nike says, "Just Do It!" Once it's done, it's done. You can take the pedal off sooner or later, but you have to get there first. After all you have nothing to lose, except a bit of rest and relaxation. Just get it done, so that when you're rich and happy, you can relax on the golf course in Hawaii, while your employees are back home working their butts off and having short lunch breaks to pay for your lifestyle, plus your new carbon fibre 3 wood that you just bought for three grand from the pro-store at the Hawaii golf club! Why buy it you ask? Because you can!

And that is my point. Once the work is done, it's done! A lot of the time it only has to be done once and the rest is just maintenance. There is no competition, only yourself and your goals. Besides most of the others are asleep anyway!

Time

There are more books and opinions on the subject of time management than I personally have been able to digest. However, time management for a lot of people means picking up breakfast on the way to work via McDonalds because they are running late.

I would like to give you my opinion on time management. So far everything you have read will ultimately free up your time by taking the steps outlined in the previous chapters. Things such as choice, accepting responsibility, taking action, self-sacrifice and discipline. Once you have overcome the challenges that are holding you back, it will free up your time so you can focus on the important things that you need to get done.

Let's say that by working on the challenges in your relationship you take action to overcome them. Then you would be happier, have a great relationship (or none), and be able to focus on your goals! This is because your mind will be able to think clearly instead of lying awake at night stewing over the fact that you're unhappy in your present relationship or situation.

Your time, besides your health, is really the most important thing in life and understanding how to use and value your time is critical.

You can always get another job. You can always get

more money. But you can never get more time! Once it is gone, it's gone. It amazes me to see people wasting hours in a day and not realising it. I have only discovered the importance of my time over the past two years, and interestingly enough my net worth quadrupled when I allocated time to building wealth. So, if what you are about to read sounds like you, then you may need to make the suggested changes more than anyone.

Does this sound like you?

It's warm and cosy and you're in a beautiful dream and then it happens - ER,ER,ER,ER,ER,ER,ER,ER,ER. It's that bloody alarm clock cranking out at full tilt. It's the most irritating buzzing noise, so you roll over and it's 6am. After you bashed the guts out of the snooze button for 27-minutes, you surface to realise it's Monday morning. From the moment you awaken, the warm cosy feeling of comfort is taken away by the alarm clock. You realise that when you were asleep, your challenges in life were gone. But now you wake to the reality and the outcome of your previous choices in life.

After rushing to get ready for work, because you snoozed for another 27-minutes, all the while deferring your responsibilities, you hop in the car. As you turn on the ignition, you see the low fuel light come on and you swear because you just spilt coffee from your travel mug on your white clothes as you climbed into your leased motor car. And, not happy, off to work you go. Then as you walk in to work and mumble 'morning,' as if you cared, to all the other 'employees,' who deep down you have nothing in common with except the fact that you're all grumpy on Mondays. As you progress through your day, it eventually gets to 5pm and you might even do some overtime without pay, as you are snowed under with a whole heap of work.

Then you drive home at an average speed of 17 km/ph because everyone else decided to leave to go home from work at the same time as you did. It is then that you start to question whether the $30,000 you outlaid on the lease for your sporty car was worth it, as you never seem to get over 17 km/ph. On arrival home at 6pm you put on your comfy couch clothes, and cook for an hour and then clean up for another half hour. You then zone yourself out in front of the idiot box until you pass out and wake up dribbling out of the corner of your mouth. Realizing reality still exists you shuffle off to the bedroom where you pretend life's realities can disappear for your 10 hour oversleep session.

Then Tuesday morning at 6am … ER,ER,ER,ER,ER,ER, ER,ER. Time to belt the crap out of that poor little alarm clock again! Today is a better day because you have dinner at Mum's (or maybe it's at your mother-in-law's) every Tuesday and she is cooking your favourite roast.

Then by Wednesday, you have made it through the halfway mark, Thursday is late night shopping, so you choose to go to the shopping centre and crank out the Visa card and shop until it's full of clothes and ornaments that'll collect dust. You stop shopping when your Visa gets to its limit again.

But then all of a sudden it's Friday. You wake up happier than normal, you seem to be in a better mood and so does everyone else at work. You have a laugh or two and then that afternoon it's payday. You call past the ATM on the way home and you get excited for a brief moment as your account balance comes out showing your pay packet in your account.

All of a sudden you have money in the bank and it feels good! Then you come to the realisation that your pay is spent before you even got it to pay off the Visa card loaded up with lots of stuff, stuff that in the long run gets you stuff all! So you pull out some cash because it's time to celebrate after a big week at work. After all you deserve to, don't you? Well then it's off to the pub or the video shop where you drown your reality in alcohol and eat potato wedges filled with oil and salt, or alternatively hire five videos and order in pizza.

Then you go into pretend mode over the weekend, passing time with videos or suffering through a hangover that you're paying interest on.

Then it starts all over again! Monday morning ... at 6am ... ER, ER, ER, ER, ER, ER, ER, ER, ER. And you repeat the same habits over and over and over and over!

Some people think by changing jobs that all their problems will be solved, but you need to understand that going to work is a habit you chose to undertake, and the main reason you are there is most probably to collect a pay packet. If you can get paid for doing something you love, then that is definitely a bonus. Statistics show 83% of the working population does not enjoy what they do for a living. The main reason most go to work is to earn money by selling time, but understand the difference between when you love doing something so much you will do it for free at the start, then the money just seems to follow. Interesting, but I promise you it's true.

Working is not the only way to generate income, and if you weren't so busy working in your job (and by the way job stands for 'just over broke'!) making someone else rich, then maybe you would have the time to make some cash in other ways. That is, ways other than selling your time for $10-15/hour!

Another thing I often hear is people who think their job is a good one to have because they are highly paid. Things like, *"I'm doing well, and I'm on a $100,000/year package."* Whoop dee doo, that's success, is it? No way. While they're off earning $100,000/year by working 70-hours a week, they also have a weight problem so big, that even a good weight loss centre can't help! And to top it off, they probably also have a relationship that is about to become a divorce statistic. Not to mention the huge leases on the cars and a house with a stack of unused equity in it.

So are they successful?

I really don't care whether you're on $20,000 or $100,000/year. Most people think their problem is that they don't have enough money, and they also think they don't have any spare time. Well get off the grass and realise that we all have 24-hours a day and 365-days a year. It hasn't changed since I can recall, so the obvious question you need to ask yourself is, *"What are you choosing to do with your time?"*

Consider your weekly-take-home pay. Don't bother about before tax figure as the money for tax is already gone. Work out what time you wake up and then what time you pull in your driveway. Now let's say you get up at 6-am right? And you get home at 6pm right? Then isn't that a 12-hour day. Now you say, *"Yeah but I am only at work for eight hours of that,"* and that's exactly my point!

If you didn't have the job, you could get up and go straight to work on yourself. If you didn't have the job, working for the boss you don't like and surrounding yourself with other employees that you find to be generally negative people, then you would have your 12-hours a day back for yourself to build your own empire, instead of building the company owner's or shareholder's empires.

Now what is your weekly take-home pay? Let's say for this example it's $600-per week. Then add up all your hours, including time in the car and overtime as well. (Remember: if you didn't have the job then you wouldn't have to spend the time in the car travelling to and from work!). If it comes to 60-hours per week then divide that by your take-home pay. The reality is that the rate of pay you accept is just $10/hour, and folks that **is** the only figure that counts!

So let me illustrate it in this way:

- Net take home pay (after tax) = $600.00/week
- Total hours from home to home = 60 hours/week
- Divide your net pay by total hours = $10.00/hour
- And that is your actual wage per hour! = $10.00/hour

And don't go spouting off when you get a pay rise or a bonus, just add them on to your previous wages and work out your new hourly rate. If it goes from $10/hour to $12/hour then I wouldn't be doing back flips down the road in excitement. Seems to me that most people have pre-empted what it is they are going to spend or have already spent their pay rise or bonus anyway.

The only time I would bother to get a little excited would be if you decided to buy some blue chip shares with your bonus, or save the pay rise for a deposit on an investment property. Otherwise you will just increase your means of living to 108% of your new income.

The questions you need to ask yourself are these. What price am I selling my time for, and am I spending my time in the most productive way for me? The other question to ask yourself is the following. Is there something I can do or offer that creates an income stream where I am not selling my time for an hourly rate?

So now that I have just made you feel lousy about being an employee where do you go from here? If you're going to be, or need to be an employee for the short-term, then do it so you can get paid to learn about an industry you may want to get involved in.

For example, if you want to learn about real estate but are

working at a chicken factory, then go and put time and energy into getting a job as a property manager or real estate sales person, and get paid by someone else to make mistakes and learn on their behalf! Do it on someone else's money not yours. The only other reason you would hold a job, in my opinion, is to qualify for finance for investment loans, as this is what I did. It's a bit of a challenge to convince a bank to lend you money if you don't have a job!

Although in saying this it's getting easier to find non-conforming lenders on real estate, who don't care if you have a job or not, and are prepared to lend you money, but you will also find that they may only lend to 80% of the property value where as a traditional bank may go to 95% of the property value, but this can also vary from country to country.

So am I telling you to quit your job tomorrow? YES, well almost, you may need to sort a few things out first as discussed in previous chapters!

Now let's look at your current time schedules. Or don't you have one? It is simple and it comprises of two parts.

Firstly, write down on a piece of paper each day what you **have** to do for the day. Then write down what time each task starts and finishes. Don't worry about writing down 'going to the pub,' I'm talking about compulsory short or long-term tasks such as work, exercise, walking the dogs etc. For example:

MONDAY:

6:00 am	Wake up
7:15 am	Leave for work
8:10 am	Arrive at work
5:15 pm	Leave work

6:10 pm	Arrive home
6:10 pm	Cook dinner
7:20 pm	Finish dinner and wash dishes
7:30 pm	Jog with the dog
7:40 pm	Home and shower
8:00 pm	Finish shower and now your free time begins!

Now of course your situation may vary, you may have kids on your daily routine list, or other duties like football coaching or a netball game, but I think you get the concept. Do this for one complete week.

Now what time do you want to go to bed? Is it 11:30pm or 1:00am? Work out how much sleep you need. In my opinion, 6 to 7 hours is more than enough. Then do it for every day including the weekend. Leave out all the mindless tasks like cleaning the house and washing the car, just put in the major things you will be continuing to do for the short-term. Now I know that things like socializing can be hard to determine how much time they will consume. They may depend on who rings up on the weekend and invites you around for the BBQ or to watch the football match, but I make sure I socialize with all my friends and family regularly.

Now add up all the hours you have from the beginning of your free time until bedtime. What is your answer? 28-hours per week? Is it more or maybe less? I have seen this go into the minus for some people. Now I'm not saying that this is the way you have to plan your time, for now it is just a method of identifying where your time is going. Another great way of finding out where your time is going is to write down what you spend every fifteen minutes of each day doing. Granted it's a little tedious, but it is effective.

Here's my point!

If you are not allocating your free time each week to follow your dreams and desires, doing the important things rather than the urgent things eg. to build wealth or spend time with your partner or kids then until you choose to quit your job, you won't ever have enough time to do what should be done, rather than doing what shouldn't be done. I am also giving you permission to pay people to clean your house, do your ironing, wash your cars and cook if you want to. If you can hire these people for ten bucks an hour why bother doing it yourself? They probably want the money, and in the time it saves you, you can go to work on the important things in life.

As a single 27-year old, I have built a property portfolio of over $5 million in 2-years as an average paid employee, and generated great positive cash flow. The only way it was done was by allocating time and energy after hours to building wealth. Once I had put the time into one property deal and the transaction was completed then I didn't have to do it again. The rent is continually paid and I own the house for as long as I want to. Now obviously this is a form of leverage as well. I buy it once and rent comes in every week forever, and that is basic leverage. But I had to choose to do it, it took self-discipline, and I had to sacrifice a few things along the way, but it was worth it.

I believe the biggest factor in time consumption in every house I ever enter is TV. Now I think TV has its place. It can be fun to watch at times, but let's face it, if you need to miss out on it for a year or two is it really going to kill you? I doubt it!

The only reason I am wealthy at a young age is because I do things other people don't. So now I can do what other people can't! Hey, remember this quote, it came from my close friend Peter Noble: **'success is not convenient but the rewards are'.**

I have only ever met one person who has implemented this next plan, but he is now worth over a million bucks!

Go to your local supermarket and grab the biggest box you can find. Take it home and unplug your television (or three of them if you have one in each room!) and put them into the box. Then get a newspaper and scrunch up the pages and fill the box with packing and paper until it's full. Take rolls of packing tape and wrap the television box up using all the rolls of tape. And use obscene amounts of tape!

Then take it to your shed or your friend's house and put it in the back corner and stack everything you can on top of it including a lawnmower and the old couch. Now lock the shed and give the key to your housemate, partner or friend. From now on when you come home you can cash in your free time for useful tasks that will improve your life, or other people's, without being distracted by the argument on some cheap TV soapie!

Once your television is gone you can focus 100% on your productivity. Now you can go on your merry way of getting the important stuff done. You may read books, listen to tapes or start a business from home. You may spend time with your partner. And no, spending time with your partner doesn't mean sitting on the couch veging every night. I mean actually communicating with them, setting goals or maybe even going to the movies together if that's what you both enjoy. The time you spend with your partner may be two hours a fortnight that is pre-planned and something to look forward to, versus what a lot of people do by spending four hours a night on the couch dozing in and out of consciousness whilst smoking. You may visit friends or family or spend time with your pets. The list goes on and on, but once the house is peaceful without the daily 'armed hold-ups' being belted out across the lounge room and down the hallway into each room on the 6 o'clock news –

it's a lot easier to focus on what is really important and in your control!

Don't even bother with watching the news. It's just history anyway. It's about things that have happened, nothing you can do or say is going to change those things. It is only what you do today that is going to make you and the world a better place tomorrow. TV is just a media business, and it makes the owners and shareholders wealthy by selling advertising. So if you want to own your slice of TV then buy some shares in Newscorp, as they own most of the TV stations anyway! As for newspapers, aren't they in the box in the shed with the TV in it? Good! So you now have my opinion of the newspaper as well! It's a pity newspaper isn't softer then we could use it for toilet paper!

The next thing to do is follow these two simple procedures. For a more detailed insight I suggest reading the book 'First Things First' by Stephen Covey. But I'm going to give you my shortened version...

There are only two decisions you ever need to make, in my opinion, with regard to your time management:

1:    IS IT IMPORTANT?

2:    IS IT URGENT?

So let me elaborate. When you wake up Monday morning to go to work, is it important that you go or just urgent? Well in my opinion it's urgent, because if you don't go you will get sacked and not be able to maintain your lease payments on your car.

But is it really important that you go? Well, only for today. How is attending work going to assist you in the long-term as you travel down the highway of life, trying to achieve good things for yourself and help others? That's right, it's not. The company (and I have seen it done) could turn around tomorrow and make you redundant, and then all of a sudden the work you were doing that was urgent at the time has no value to you. Plus, when you're made redundant your care factor for the company ends up at zero anyway!

If you had been allocating time and energy today to building your wealth portfolio up for tomorrow, then does it matter when the corporate boss flies down from interstate to make you redundant? No, because you did what was important with your time when you could, rather than doing unpaid overtime to make the company owner or shareholder rich.

Besides, when the corporate boss of the zoo you work for, comes down to lay you off, ask them when the last time they watched their son at football training was? He will probably say something along the lines of, *"I haven't seen him at football practice for three months because I have been so flat out travelling for work lately."* That's the sort of answer you seem to get from urgent people.

Gee, I really hope the career, or redundancy payout, is worth it, because even though it's important to spend time with your kids, for some reason when you're working for someone else it seems that urgent tasks always pop up! But only if you choose to let them!

So if important issues are things like:

- Staying fit to avoid heart disease
- Giving two hours of your time a month to a charity
- Spending time on your wealth creation or building up your home-based business

Then, why are so few people doing anything important with their time?

It's OK to say no to a few birthday parties or weddings

and holiday trips. If you need to sacrifice every now and then, so be it. It all comes back to one point my Dad made clear to me from a very young age, *'If you want something bad enough you will get it!'* And by knowing what you want, and having the time to do it now - you can go and get it. But remember every hour to ask yourself, *"Is what I am currently doing urgent or is it important?"* By doing this you will soon have time management under control!

Use a diary for appointments, just a manual one that cost ten dollars. It doesn't have to be some electric gizmo with a spreadsheet and camera on it. A diary and a pencil is a good place to start. The shortest pencil is better than the longest memory, so if you write it down you will remember it. Take note of what you do from now on with your time. Remember to ensure you are doing important things with your time. Avoid urgent things wherever possible. If it's urgent enough then it becomes important and it will be done anyway. That's as complicated as time management needs to be, in my opinion!

Chapter 7

Singular Focus

Singular focus. It works in the simplest way, but has a powerful effect. If you have stuff in your life that needs to be done because it is either holding you back or needs to be attended to, then the way to eliminate it out of your life is exactly that. Elimination.

Let's say, for example, you had the following challenges in your life:

- Credit card debt
- A car to sell
- Messy financial records
- Unhappy employment
- Too poor investments in shares

But on a positive note, you would like to do the following things as well in the short term:

- Read up on property investing
- Attend a real-estate investment seminar
- Join a gymnasium or hire a personal trainer lessons
- Take the kids on a short, but fun holiday somewhere

Tackle it like this. Take a pen and paper and write down everything that's at loose ends. Down to the smallest detail like changing the postal address on your driver's licence.

Then take one issue that is annoying or costing you time or money. When you have free time, focus on your task, one challenge at a time and follow through with physical action until you have overcome it. Even if it takes two weeks to solve one issue, it's OK. Your list will reduce and eventually you will have done all the things that were taking up space. Remember to clean out your wardrobe and give your old clothes to charity, then you have made your donation for the month and you have given something to someone less fortunate, so now something is on its way in return to you!

By focusing singularly on each issue at a time, you will get through to the bottom of your list a lot faster. You will also be a lot clearer about your new direction, as you won't have clutter clogging up your headspace. You then can focus on the important issues that will give you some benefits over time. Perhaps like the ones I listed above. Your list may well be different but I think you get the point. Simple enough? I thought so!

Chapter 8

Money

Well, the topic of money always seems to open a few cans of worms! It amazes me to hear so many opinions about money and investing, yet 96% of people simply don't have any money or investments. They are not speaking from a point of competence! So, do yourself a big favour, when it comes to the subject of money, only take advice from someone who's got it. Not your accountant, financial advisor, or insurance salesperson as they are just employees. I'm talking about taking advice from rich people and rich people only.

And don't say you don't know any ... Advice can come from a book, tape or seminar, or even the Internet can be pretty handy these days as well – but make sure your source is credible. Of course, there are varying opinions amongst the rich about the best vehicle to create wealth, but they do have the one ingredient in common that counts, CASH! And the more they have the better. If you want to hang out with rich people, buy their books and tapes, visit their websites, attend their seminars and stuff in as much information as you can until you can't get anymore in.

OK, so now we know where to go for good advice, let's move on ...

Money is just an idea and it's just how you perceive it to

be, as to the reality of it. You see, if you drop a $100 note on the ground and a dog walks up and sniffs it, the only thing the dog is likely to do is to cock his leg on it. The dog doesn't bark off to his mates, *"Hey look guys I just found a hundred bucks."* So why is this? Well it's a thing called perceived value. As humans, we believe a $100 note to be worth $100, but in reality it's worth about 20-cents to make at the mint, and even less to the dog, as money doesn't exist in a dog's world.

So now we understand perception, then why do 96% of us perceive money as a hard thing to attract? Is there a shortage? No way, there is over a million dollars each if you evenly divide the wealth of the world amongst everyone on the planet! So why is everyone concerned about a shortage of money all the time? I believe it's because of what people perceive to be true. Money is abundant, but before it's going to come into your wallet, you need to accept that there is a ton of the stuff out there and it will come to you if you allow it to.

In this day and age, it is basically impossible to survive through the physical plane of life without money. And by surviving I mean food, shelter, medical treatment and so on. 96% of people have this theory that money doesn't make you happy. Well whoever says that is plain broke! If I were going to be unhappy, I would rather do it in a Porsche than on a pushbike! And I know money can't buy love and happiness, but if I was going to be unhappy I would much rather be rich and unhappy, than poor and unhappy.

So what is it that money can provide for you? It gives you choices, like the choice to wake up whenever you want to, donate to charities when you want to, rather than when you can afford too. It buys luxury items to have a load of fun with your friends, the choice of whether or not you have to go to work and most of all it gives you freedom of time to do what you want!

So why do people get so offended around the subject of money? I don't have the answer, except that they have a set of beliefs that were conditioned in their mind, based upon historical external influences (such as their parents) and poor money management.

Please understand, times are changing and things are moving at ten times the pace, today. The days of $40,000/year being a good income are over; rather $40,000/month would be a good starting point.

This book is not simply about investing financially, but more so to encourage you to invest in yourself first, because then you will get the financial results you desire. I believe that firstly you need your head to be in the right spot, and accepting that cash, and lots of it, is a good thing to have. If you can't 'get over it' that money is a great thing to have, then stay broke. But don't come crying to me when you're 65-years old and need to rely on a pension for income!

I do need to mention, however, that money is a very important tool to help you achieve self-satisfaction. A rich person can help a lot of people, but a poor person can help no one. It's pretty sad that school teaches kids to get a job, but forgets to educate them on money management, especially considering the reason most go to work is to earn income. It's no wonder Robert Kiyosaki has done so well with his 'Rich Dad' series of educational information on the subject of money. And good on him too!

It's probably fair to say that there is a market place requiring education on the subject of money, which is limited only by the population of the world! I bet that could be a business opportunity! Especially if you think of almost every person in the world who has attended school and then gone out and got a job with an income – most have had no formal education on the topic of money.

Chapter 9

Association

The biggest problem some of you could have with the issue of association is that you may have to get rid of some of the people in your life! When you discover the real power that associating with others can have on you, you will know why I say this!

No matter how hard you try, other people are going to have an influence on you in some way. It will be either negative or positive. Take your friends and family for example; if they're anything like most, they always have opinions on what is right for you to do with your life and your business affairs.

Now when I say business affairs I am talking about you. Start looking at and treating yourself as if you are a business entity. 'You incorporated' that is your business! You need to learn to make your 'business' decisions based on what's best for you, not what your friends and family believe is best for you!

Your associations will try to influence your decisions and choices on anything and everything, for example, like whether you should leave your job, a particular investment decision, a part-time business you want to start up and run from home. Ultimately, while these people don't usually, or intentionally, mean you any harm by trying to enforce their opinions on you, by doing what they recommend, you may end up harming yourself!

Our associates base their opinions on what they know and assume is the right thing to do in life, however, there are many parents today, still wanting their kids to go to university and get a good job. But then what? Pay your home off? Work 'til retirement and play bowls? I think we all know that's not the key to success. Yeah sure, there's a place for university, but don't confuse it with a set of beliefs or limited knowledge on maximizing wealth and income generation!

Association is everywhere you go. It is in the street, at work, in our homes, and on the idiot box. Everywhere you go you are associating with people at various levels throughout your daily life.

It happens as we pass people in the street and they smile or frown, when we buy lunch from a café and have people surrounding us, as well as via the radio in the car and the music we play.

On the journey of continual self-fulfilment, we can change our external influences and choose what we want to take on board as advice. We can learn to respect, but disregard, the opinions of most, and choose whose opinions we will be influenced by.

For example, this book is simply my opinion. You can choose to accept it and be influenced by it if you wish, but it comes back to your choice!

I remember when I first got involved with a network marketing company; I used to attend meetings every Monday night. There would be a few hundred or so people in the room each week, all looking for more out of life and the energy was always positive. There were always successful business builders in the room who were wealthy, not only financially, but mentally as well. After the meeting you could talk with the successful ones and learn how to build your own business. They would always be happy to help and the association was always beneficial in some positive way. Then I would roll into work the next day all fired up from the great associations at the meeting the night before, and feel like I was now associating with the members of my local zoo!

It really is amazing how much of an effect people can have on us. Personally, I am continually assessing who and what I am spending my time on. People seem to have a habit of bringing you to their level. People with high levels of motivation and energy will pick you up and people with low levels of energy and negative influences drag you down. Some people will just use you and call you when it suits them or when they need something and others will consume all your time, because they have nothing better to do.

If you find you are a leader by nature or character and that others are attracted to you, they may find you a positive influence to hang around and therefore, they feel good by being around you.

Personally I do not read much of the newspaper, except of course for the real estate section! I'm not saying it's wrong to read the newspaper, that's just my choice. I find that the first twenty pages are always negative and just instil more fear into me, but I do read the financial section, and the social sections can be fun too.

I rarely watch TV except for sport, as I enjoy sport. If you have a favourite show then watch it, but turn it off after the show has finished and get back onto building yourself. I believe, if you can avoid the news as well, you will be doing yourself a favour as it is usually very negative.

You see, the power of association is not to be mistaken as being in the shape of people only. It can also be the environment you are in. If you hang around a bar or club where head blowing music and drugs are in high use, then you are not likely to walk out of there feeling like you can do front flips down the footpath!

Sure, some disillusioned people think that these sorts of places are OK, but I think you get my point. It's pretty hard to leave a club like this and go home feeling positive about life.

As you travel along on your success rocket to your destination, you will find all sorts of punters trying to hold you back. 99% of the time they are just space junk and when they see you heading off with vision, direction and a destination, they think that holding you back is easier to do than to get their own rocket and learn to ride it. So they may use verbal, physical and or emotional blackmail (even unintentionally, sometimes) to keep you from progressing, because this way they can remain safe in their comfort zone and not feel insecure by losing you. This happens in relationships, business and families all the time. This is why I believe that associations can have a strong influence as to why you may not be achieving your plans.

It's only natural for people to let their associations affect them! But as we associate with others all day and everyday, we must understand why it is so important to realise how we can be so easily affected by these associations.

One of the underlying influences behind what people say and do is their beliefs. Beliefs are so jammed into some people's minds that you won't change them. They cover everything from religion, money, relationships, education, investing, fitness, diet and the list goes on. People seem to have a thousand different beliefs around these topics and as you head on your way aboard the success rocket of life, you will also generate your own beliefs. This is what ultimately equals your direction and destination.

The best way to get your beliefs straightened out is to find an expert. For example, when it comes to my physical training and health, I use Australian fitness coach, Ian King. He has coached Olympic athletes from various sports and his name has been plastered all over Men's Health magazines. On the subject of money and investing in real estate, I got my ideas from Dolf de Roos, and a number of others. No matter what I was trying to achieve I always made sure I associated with the best people and the best minds.

I didn't care about the price, as I just needed the information and I needed it then and there. It was certainly a short cut, and at the time it seemed extravagant, but now I realise it was the best thing I did. People used to cringe at the prices I paid to get around the best people possible, and now they cringe at the high level of results I have achieved. The point is simply that the association is what is most important.

Of course the information is great, but like I said earlier, association is everywhere. If it meant I had to get good association by putting on my Ian King fitness video rather than watching the news, then at least the influence and association was positive and was heading me in the direction I wanted to be going, rather than watching the news update on armed hold-ups!

I really want you to take a good hard look at everyone and every environment you hang around. Don't judge people materially by the car they drive, but more by what they do and say. I'm not saying never speak to them again, but you may want to assess what you discuss with them and work out if they have the capacity to digest what you just told them about your $2.2 million property development (using none of your own money and a net profit of $600,000!) and see if they respond with a common sense answer rather than a belief-system reaction.

Youth seem to be a good example of association influences. In a world where chemical drugs are becoming popular and responsibility seems like a thing of the past, youth appear to be influenced by their associates more so than anyone. Whether it is a group of kids in a car, or at a nightclub or wherever – when someone pulls out a bag of powder, it is almost not cool to be amongst the group that doesn't join in! Of course, the person taking the drugs thinks it's OK, and they have a social obligation with their peers to uphold. But do they really believe that it's OK to take something mixed with rat poison and fly spray? Seem crazy?

That's because it is!

The incompetent person with the drugs believes it's OK and because of that they try to pass that belief on. The only way to beat them is to stand your ground or not get involved with them in the first place, unless you can change them for the better.

To this day I make an effort every day to assess my association. If someone is wasting my time then I move on quickly. I only take advice if they have done it.

A friend of mine who is a world champion athlete, Brett Sands, once said to me, *"If you want it done properly, do it yourself"* and I have never forgotten that lesson.

In your financial affairs, relationship or business, if it needs fixing or work done on it, then take action and your questions to an expert and get it sorted out. Don't let people's inexperienced opinions drift you off to the same planet they are on, because you won't find your way back, as they have no idea where they are anyway. Sure, have your friends or family to lean on for support, when required, but support shouldn't be confused with advice and opinions should be just that. So next time someone tries to sell you emus, because they think it's a better investment than property just kindly say, *"Thanks for your opinion and by the way, have you thought about selling turkeys, it would match your personality better than emus!"* And besides, I don't think a bank would lend you the purchase price of an emu! Plus, emus don't rent out as well as houses do!

Chapter 10

Unemployable!

This is going to be a chapter that will really challenge a lot of people's belief systems. You often hear people talk about the good old days and how things were so different back then. Often you hear the same people say how we are so lucky to be alive today and not back in the old days when life was simple compared to today, but it was also a lot tougher back then.

We hear of the old days of slavery when a slave could work all day, 6-days a week, for food and small amounts of money with a ball and chain around their ankle so they couldn't run away. As a slave, they would be expected to hop aboard the ship and paddle in time with the Master's drumbeat.

Sounds like pain? Well it is, and there are an awful lot of people who have forgotten or fail to notice that slavery is still common practice and a legal industry today.

The concept of the ball and chain restricted its detainee from living a life of their choice as they had no rights or freedom. A slave was required to do as they were told; they had to start and finish work when told to, complete boring tasks and had to work through all types of pain. It was not only de-motivating work, but it was also physically tiring and emotionally disturbing. If they did not obey the orders given to do the work, they would be given physical discipline or the death penalty. The people in charge had to give their slaves food and basic shelter, because otherwise the slaves would die and then the Masters would be without workers to complete their tasks and do the manual labour.

In today's world, it seems to be insane that people could treat the human race like that, and thank God that the laws of today prevent atrocities, like slavery, from happening today.

Instead, the modern life progresses like this ... As we develop through childhood; we commence our formal education through the system we know as school. We leave school often to begin work or continue studying in the hope of getting a job in the field we studied. Then it is off to work we go. Often we then get married or enter a relationship, but continue working, selling our time to earn money. Then all of a sudden there is an addition to the family. Suddenly a miniature version of yourself and your partner is crawling around your ankles. Parenthood is no doubt a beautiful thing, but we seem to be missing so many of the joys that parenting can provide as we continue to head off to work as employees to earn our money. Then as the one, two or more children grow up we continue to work to pay off the home and provide for the family we created by choice. The children eventually find their own direction and move on in life and as we are heading towards our later 50s or 60s we begin to look forward to retirement. Then we turn 65 and cash in some of our retirement cheque to buy a new four wheel drive and a caravan and promptly head off on our holiday around the country that we have never seen before, because we were too busy working most of our lives!

So we set off on the retirement holiday of a lifetime, and 2-years later we are either dead or dead broke!

Now I know that not everyone retires off on a four wheel drive holiday, and it is not a bad thing to do if that is your dream, but the concept I am trying to get you to understand is that if you choose to be an employee and repeat your habits over the years and not allocate any time or energy to your future wealth then chances are you're going to require some sort of financial assistance in your retirement. So how is it if slavery is illegal that we end up living a life of existence rather than a lifetime of fulfilment?

Well it all started when we began conditioning our mind at a very young age in the schooling system that has been in place for hundreds of years. As parents we do not intentionally mean to condition our children for harm, and we do not realise that our own parents allowed us to be conditioned in the same way ... So how did we become conditioned to the way we think and the actions we take in everyday life?

Well we start off by going to school. Things like getting up every day to an alarm clock or mum or dad waking us up. Then we attend school from Monday to Friday and have weekends, holidays and public holidays off. The tests at school require us to memorize text books and often retain very little knowledge.

At the age of fifteen or sixteen when we complete our schooling years, we have the choice to either study for a few more years or get a job or perhaps a traineeship. Whether the choice is made to study or to work after leaving school, the desired outcome for someone who studies is to eventually get a job in their chosen field. As you commence your working years, or as some call them careers, you earn money by selling your time. It is then that you discover a home loan takes 25 or 30-years to pay off, so your only option is to rent, board or to buy a home.

You then progress to family life, or perhaps you decide not to have a family, because as the cost of living goes up, your pay packet won't necessarily keep pace. So maybe you decide to live your life without having a family, because then you will have a little more money to spend on yourself. After all, to earn money generally you either have to be employed or self-employed and the practice of being an employee is to sell time for money. As you continue your skill level or experience will increase and you may be able to charge a better hourly rate. As you increase your pay packet, you will have increased responsibility to go with the job. Working longer hours and harder at what you choose to do, you then spend your wages and increase your borrowings to your new income level and live at around 108% of your income.

Now you have increased your debt, you're trapped, as your kids and or other commitments for your time and money increase. You then hit retirement and, 'Yippee' it is now time to go and have a life. You deserve it, after all you have worked so hard for many years and you owe it to yourself to take a long break. Sooner or later you run out of money or purpose, and life is nearing the end.

It is still a common practice amongst most people to over spend all their lives and it really amazes me that the school system has not realized the importance of money management and other critical skill education.

I don't recall having lessons at school on money management, managing good debt versus bad debt, relationship counselling, leadership, or diet and nutrition, let alone how and why you should donate to charities, team building, business management, corporation and taxation systems, or property and share market investing. I will stop there, but you know what I mean. I am talking about classes on real life issues and things that you will have to deal with in real life outside of school.

The way we were conditioned began at around 5-years old or younger. We got into a routine and we learned about holidays. We got a small amount of pocket money and were told we could spend it at the canteen. On our next pocket money payday, it's straight off to the canteen to blow the lot on cola and ice cream. We learnt to live our pay cycle from week to week, and then as we grew older we had to do jobs to earn pocket money. We were then conditioned to sell our time for money. So as soon as we were old enough we got a job as a junior flipping burgers at a hamburger shop.

I hope you can see the pattern developing here. It is not meant be a harmful pattern. It is a good pattern, from the point of view of teaching us to work hard for our money. It taught us responsibility and required some discipline and sacrifice. But, you need to accept that you will not break free of the rut you are in by selling your time for an hourly rate. If it worked, then why are so many people broke? and more importantly, unhappy.

You see, the simple fact is that nothing has changed from the old days of slavery. We are still doing it to ourselves. The only difference between then and now is that it used to be acceptable to **have** slaves, and now we make the choice to **become** one. We prostitute our time for money and work to earn money. By putting ourselves into debt with things like cars or credit cards, we fail to realise that we are now locked into going to work to pay it back with some interest as well.

Of course, we are conditioned from our younger years to work in a routine, have weekends free and awaken each morning to the stupid invention known as an alarm clock. We receive pocket money on a weekly cycle or similar, and believe that money comes to us weekly on Thursdays. If our parents did not give us pocket money because they couldn't afford to, then we grow up thinking that money is scarce and hard to get. The first thing for someone to do to obtain money is to sell their time, as it seems to be a relatively quick way to obtain some cash and temporarily solve the problem of having no cash. We can sell our time as a child by doing jobs around the house to earn money, and so we begin the pattern and mind conditioning of selling our time. Many youth get a part-time job to have some more cash. Saving for a car is the dream for many and often our first investment of any type and also our first major liability financially.

With banks recording their record profits, they are happy to give a car loan to you if you can't pay for a car yourself and the cycle of bad debt commences. A credit card comes in the post and as you were a little short of cash this month you pay for car tyres on your credit card and the trap of consumer credit continues.

The position we end up in appears to be one of slavery, as we work and sell our time to earn money, repay debts and try to maintain our lifestyle. But we bring it on ourselves. We could point the finger all day and blame someone else, but when you point your finger, there's three fingers pointing back at yourself and it doesn't solve the problem.

The fact that our belief systems are so programmed with habits that we believe are OK to partake in, is what really lines us up to becoming a voluntary slave. Not only is being a slave bad for your soul, but it is also preventing you from becoming the best you can be. So is it that we are not aware of what we are doing with our time, or have we never taken a step back, had a good look at ourselves and realised what we are actually doing everyday? We are so conditioned to do what we do, that we don't think that there is any other option in life besides selling our time for money.

As we grow up we become more aware of things around us. When you were 2-years old, you didn't realise that you didn't know how to drive a car. Then at around 10 or so years old you realised that you knew that you didn't know how to drive a car. When you were 2-years old you were unconsciously incompetent and then at 10-years old you were consciously incompetent.

We need to be more aware of what we don't know. The fact is, because we don't believe there is any other option in life, we don't even stop to think about what else we could be doing with our time. There are so many more options. Just stop and think, maybe you don't know what the other options are, because you have never gone looking for them! After all, maybe the challenge is your lack of knowledge, rather than a lack of money.

So often we get stuck in a rut that seems to be impossible to get out of. The days of slavery are over, and yet most people (especially employees and even some self-employed people) are volunteering to be a slave for small weekly amounts of money. They are really only being slaves to themselves. No one is holding a gun to their head forcing them to do what they do.

The only difference between the old-time slavery and now is that you don't have a ball and chain swinging off your ankle and you can run from the rut, if you choose to. These days, instead of a ball and chain, you've a mortgage, a car loan or a few credit cards to slow you down. In some cases it may be your partner, children or business debts, but you are still required to wake up and sell your time to someone or something to collect money, repay your debts and maintain your existence.

So as we continue through our working years we often increase our costs and standards of living. We upgrade houses or cars, travel on borrowed money or basically just spend more than we earn. As the years go on and times seem tough continually, we become more imbedded with what we believe in and the level of ignorance increases. Then as we become more and more ignorant we stop our minds from being open to opportunity and then the struggle appears tougher again. We struggle to believe in ourselves and the vicious circle goes on. We plan to retire happy, but realise that the lack of cash prevents happiness and winding up broke after years of work doesn't help.

We may end up having no purpose to awake to and unhappiness creates illness. And sooner rather than later we may find we 'kick the bucket'. Because so many of us have seen this repeated pattern occur in other people's lives, we believe it to be the normal procedure for life and it becomes imbedded in our belief systems.

The mind is only conditioned by beliefs based on previous external and internal influence, in other words, how we let others influence us, and how we let the outcome of our own decisions impact on our belief systems. Usually influence from any source is to intentionally obtain a positive outcome for one or the other party.

If we accept that we only do what we do because of our beliefs and habits, then it should not be that hard to change them when needed. The challenge is that our beliefs are only based around what we know, not what we don't know. If I told you that in order to quit your job tomorrow, you would have to generate twice your original income immediately to live off without getting another job, then you may feel a little scared (especially with the mortgage payments to make). So how will you generate the income to survive? … Well the challenge is not how to make the money as that is the easy bit. The challenge is more in dealing with your own belief system and wondering if there is another way to make money besides selling your time.

If you do not know of any other way to generate income other than selling your time, then you will find it tough to pay those mortgage payments. The key word in what I have said above is the word, 'know'. If you do not 'know' how to generate income besides selling your time, then you will never go and do anything else but sell your time to earn money. The knowledge is the power. If you have knowledge you have power. If you know how to do something then your beliefs are strong because you know how to and probably have done so before, so you believe in yourself.

The only difference between a rich person and a poor person is that the rich know how to make and create money while the poor are off earning money. The ability and capacity most of us have is not really different. You don't have to be talented to be rich. Some say you need to be prepared to take a risk in life. But I reckon if you work 'til you're 65 for someone else, selling your time, and not investing, then that to me is risky.

I think that common sense is uncommon and if you think that taking a risk might be an expensive attitude, then try 'ignorance' – that's really expensive!

We all have the ability to be something better than a mundane employee and we can all do it. Some of course will not and others will. Take a look around at wealthy people today. Is Richard Branson an employee? What about Gerry Harvey or Donald Trump? No way! They are employees, sure, of their own companies! So could you run Virgin airlines like Richard Branson does? Maybe he had some lessons along the way whilst he was following his dream and becoming the best person he could be. I'm not suggesting setting up an airline company tomorrow, but hey, why not try if you want to!

There is nothing wrong with being a dedicated employee and if you get satisfaction out of what you do, then great. I have a close friend who is studying occupational therapy and he loves it. I wish him luck and will help him get the best results he can, whenever I can be of assistance to him.

So if you enjoy your job and want to work for an employer or continue to sell your time until you're 65 – that's fine. Just make sure you're putting money aside into more than some compulsory government superannuation fund. If you don't know where to start then find some books written by rich people. If you are stuck in a job and a rut only maintaining your existence, then it is basically the equivalent of being in prison.

Let me show you an example.

Let's say you're working in an office, and you sit at a desk with four walls around you and maybe a window or two. You are basically in a jail and why I say this is as follows.

What if you decided to get up from your desk and leave your city because you felt like getting out of the cold weather? And what would happen if you didn't come back for 11-weeks, or tell anyone where you were going or for how long? Chances are your employers will probably stop paying you and you wouldn't have a job to come back to! You start and finish work when they tell you to, eat when they decide it's lunch time and not when your stomach says so. You do overtime unpaid, because it shows that you're a dedicated employee for giving your time for free and that proves you're passionate about the company! What a twisted way we think!

Now folks that is **slavery**! I don't care what you do for a living. Unless you are doing it because you love it, and you fly out of bed in the morning and can't wait to get to work, then you are a slave to the system! If you look forward to coming home from holidays and can't wait to get back to work then you are a very rare breed indeed. The reality is that you will not become free or rich being a standard employee or even an un-motivated self-employed person.

Unless you invest in other things that generate or create money for you, you will not become wealthy. To help create extra wealth, you could invest in business, property or shares. But understand the first investment you need to make is in yourself, in the form of knowledge.

If you have a business that is struggling, then invest in business coaching or system implementation. Look at franchising your company or employing smart people. Henry Ford admitted he was not smart, but he knew how to find smart people. If you need to invest income into property or shares then start today. I don't care if it is $20/week in a savings account. The reality is that $20/week is more than most put away, so you are ahead of the pack already! I don't care how much you earn. It is how much you keep that matters.

Someone who earns $25,000/year and invests $4,000/year is better off than someone who earns $100,000 year and invests nothing. There are a small percentage of high wage earners in the world on big incomes. Take for example a president of a company, general manager or someone who owns a good business. They may have more income than the average, but if they do not put away some money and invest it then they only have income for as long as they are selling their time.

If I had to go and get a job tomorrow I would only work for a successful company. I would want to know that someone like Richard Branson, John Singleton, Gerry Harvey or Donald Trump owned it. I would take note of the systems and training for the staff and I would keep learning and gaining knowledge as fast as possible. I would work in an industry that I wanted to learn about and I would perform at my best. I would be excited about going to work, to learn but not to earn. I would not be planning on being there forever, as my plan would be to become big myself and the time would come when my hours were too precious to give away to another empire. I would then move on to build my own empire and become the best I could be.

The drive to be better every day and to help as many other people as I can, keeps me going. Education is only knowledge but when it's applied knowledge it becomes powerful. It attracts good energy and usually a wad full of cash too!

So if you are working today and hate it, realise you need to challenge yourself for you, and not wait for an employer to do it for you. If you're dissatisfied with what you're doing then change what you do and if nothing else, get some useful knowledge.

As you may have gathered, I am unemployable and the reason is simply that it costs me too much to go to work. I miss opportunities everywhere and if I'm selling my time to someone else then they require my energy and time. All the money and lessons that I will miss out on are too costly for the sake of a pay packet.

I don't do what I do for the money; I do it so I have

purpose. I wake up and want to fire up and get going. I look forward to every day and even Monday is a great day. Every day above ground is a good day and I am going to give it my best. I am trying to be the best I can and help others along the way. I encourage my friends and family to invest continually and not for the money, but to teach them about managed risk, to push them out of their comfort zone. It allows me to help others smash their belief systems and put new beliefs in their mind. They can then become better for it, and because they believe more in themselves they then encourage others to invest in their lives as well. The world then becomes a happier place, and I can rest assured that my presence on earth has made a difference and I know that I have left a trail of success and fulfilment!

The hardest belief to break about not being an employee is that every week someone is not going to be putting wages into a bank account. I seem to be able to pay myself whenever I choose to, depending on how hard I want to work on myself and how quickly I want to generate some more money, but when I do get paid, it is usually a lot of money or a priceless lesson!

Chapter 11

Whatever It Takes!

In the busy lives so many of us seem to lead, it really does appear tough to break through to achieve what we want. It feels like a continual up-hill battle with so many running the other way! You might be tempted to question whether you are heading in the right direction or not. I agree that it may feel this way but try looking at it from a different point of view. If you're not going to do something to change where you are currently at, then where are you going to end up? If you keep doing the same things over and over, repeating the same habits over and over, then the fact is you will keep getting the same results!

I believe so many of us have got confused about what is important in life versus what appears to be important, but really isn't. Remember that 'urgent' things are different to 'important' things. First things first and do today what will make a difference tomorrow!

Sure, enjoy the moment and have a lot of fun, but you can do that anyway no matter what you are doing at the time. So no, I am not for a minute saying that every living moment should be spent on success and achieving. Quiet time out doing nothing is healthy and so is relaxation, but so few of us seem to have a spare three months to go sit on a beach with no phones to eat coconuts and oysters.

What I am saying is that if you want to achieve anything of significance then it is going to require a certain amount of energy in the right areas.

Today, more than ever before, there is a lot of help in all areas of life. Adult education is a growing industry and more and more people are realizing that what we learnt at school is not always relative to life. I get my coaching and advice from experts all around the globe. I always look for someone with outstanding results within their field.

I have spoken about several successful people that I have looked up to as mentors and as coaches. An important thing to understand is that the information and the people are out there to help. If you want free help then go to your local library. If you want to get around the people then attend their seminars or workshops. They all charge, but most of them can't charge what they are worth because no one would go to them! They all enjoy helping other people and they all get a kick out of seeing someone achieve something as a result of their influence. The reason I put emphasis on adult education is because knowledge is power. If you have knowledge you can achieve a lot, but without it you can't go very far.

Life knowledge seems to pay off so much more than Year Eight history lessons. If you feel like you are uncertain about what steps to take, then start with self-education, if nothing else. You will need to be aware of one other thing, and that is to be prepared to *"Do whatever it takes!"*

I am writing this book at 1:53am on a Tuesday morning, and I need to be up at 7am, but if that is what is required to get it done then so be it. I want it bad enough so I am prepared to make the sacrifice and have the discipline to stay up and do it. No matter what area needs improving, you are going to feel like there is a wall in front of you at times.

I am far from expert on a lot of topics, but I do know where to go to find the experts. Then all that is required is to go and take action. Even simple things like maintaining fitness. It always seems hard for a lot of people to get out of bed that little bit earlier to go for a run. The fact is that many last no more than two days at it and then complain about the lack of results, or search for a faster way to get the desired outcome. If you need to create new habits then try it for 21 days straight!

A friend of mine, Phillip Chamberlain, once said to me, *"If you do something for 21 days then it becomes a habit."* Now I remember saying this to my Dad, and he was a smoker for 42 years and he gave up by breaking the habit for more than 21 days!

Sure, you can use nicotine patches or tablets, but it still is a habit that needs to be broken. By breaking it down into daily achievable goals you will find it more realistic to achieve. To say things like, *"I will be a millionaire by the end of the year,"* is a statement, but to make it a goal we need to know how to get there and what all the steps in between are going to be.

You can look at it this way ... If "G" is the goal then $A+B+C+D+E+F = G$ and all that counts is you doing step A first then step B second and so on until you reach your goal. Write your true goals down and date them and review them frequently. I see so many people with dreams that they would like to become goals but they are unfit or have no money management skills; they work long hours for their employers or they consume junk food or smoke. Well then, how could they possibly achieve their goals?

Something is going to have to change! **Goals are just**

dreams with dates on them.

I have found that life became easier when I made my goals become part of my life. I wanted to be fit, so I now make exercise part of my daily routine. This keeps me healthy and gives me the energy I require to stay awake and push through a big day. I review my finances **daily** and my wealth continually grows. I keep in contact with my parents and all my friends weekly. I stay involved in my sporting club and donate to a charity every month.

Now these tasks are no longer goals, they are now just important parts of my day-to-day life. I don't even have to think about doing it as it comes naturally now, but I did have to set goals at the start. I still have goals, but they are different ones now. They are now related to what I want to achieve for myself or to help others, rather than what needs to be done or should have been done anyway.

I make mistakes continually, but I pick myself up and go again. If I can't pick myself up then I quickly find a seminar to attend or I plug in a tape of someone I admire and listen to his or her message. It's not always a happy and easy journey. There are tough times and there are times when emotion takes over. It's about going through those and accepting that it is all part of the journey. Just go through it and come out the other side refreshed and ready to tackle your challenges again!

You set the pace, not anyone else. If you're put in the situation where you are forced to go and achieve something then that will just push you to the next level. We are capable of so much more than we believe. No one has come close to knowing the full capacity of what we can achieve. If you have a functional mind, you can get anything you put your mind to. Even if you are physically or otherwise challenged in some way then you definitely can achieve anything, as your understanding for sacrifice and discipline is better than the average person!

No matter what it takes, if you have to get up early or stay up late to get whatever it is done, then so-be-it. If you need to fly across the country then do it. I don't care what you have to do, but if you are serious about what needs to be done then just do it and stop procrastinating.

The only thing you will miss is a bit of sleep or TV. It won't kill you and besides, once it's done it's done (a lot of the time). If you believe you deserve it, go out and get it!

If you don't, you're depriving yourself. Not helping others is depriving them of the guidance or lessons that someone once gave you. Why can't you leave the world a better place than you found it?

So step up, and be counted and go out and get what you want. It is not about once-off or short-lived motivation alone, but how to stay motivated and have passion for life. If you're achieving visible results and sticking to your tasks for more than a day or two then it is a lot easier to stay motivated. I think a lot of people don't give themselves a chance. Remember, it may take 21 days. Go, try it and see for yourself. Read a book for 20 minutes a day and I bet you get through it in 21 days! Exercise everyday for 21 days and you will be a lot fitter and you may loose some weight too! It won't kill you.

Just give yourself a chance. If you're finding it hard to do the important stuff in life, I recommend sacrificing the useless tasks you do in daily life and pay someone to do the ironing. Do the productive things for you, and pay for unproductive things to be done. Don't wash the car, clean the house or even cook; pay someone for these things as they will cost as little as $10 per hour. For $40 per week, you may be able to free up 10-hours that you were spending doing all the mind numbing chores around the home.

Go and try it, I dare you!

Chapter 12

What Now?

The previous chapters you have read are written as a description of some of the steps I have taken to allow me to achieve my desired results. Whilst acquiring money and assets is often my goal, it is really about becoming the person who **has** the money and assets. I relate achieving financial success as no different to achieving results in a sport or even successfully raising kids, for that matter. I hope the content has been relevant to you in ways that have been of assistance. I appreciate you taking your time to read this book and I want to remind you that you are a special person and have great things to offer.

Each chapter is basically about the steps I took to become wealthy, not just financially, but also mentally, emotionally and physically wealthy. My reasons for getting off my backside and doing something about my financial position was because the pain of doing what I had been doing, became too much. As I said in an earlier chapter, there are only two types of pain and that is, 'the pain of discipline' and the 'pain of regret.' I had no other choice but to become wealthy to eliminate the massive pain of being poor and unhappily employed. I needed to do whatever it took, to change the position I was in.

Many times I wanted to quit along the way. I had friends tell me I was doing things wrong with investing and I had few people with whom I could share my frustrations and challenges. I lost money on several occasions attempting various business ventures and the good old stock market, (but I have never lost money on a real estate transaction) and in a sense it has been a bit lonely trying to get ahead. But there are a lot of people out there that I now help to achieve results. I love to motivate others and they are now keeping me company! I enjoy helping others and seeing them get life-fulfilling results. Whether it be water-ski coaching or wealth coaching, I get a buzz out of seeing someone else get a result.

The first things you need to decide is what you believe are your priorities. Get them in order first as they reflect your values. If water-skiing is more of a priority than building wealth, then you will become a great water-skier. If that is your goal, then go for it. If money is not a priority, then that is your choice. For me, money seemed to be and still is the driving force behind what I want to achieve.

I'm driven by things such as having my time to myself, being free to travel, helping others, donating to charities, becoming an athlete, enjoying luxuries and so on. And they all require cash to do them!

I can't imagine life without all the wonderful experiences that money can provide. If riding camels in Egypt is what you want to do, then how much cash will it require to do that? There are ways to work and get paid to enjoy it at the same time. Find a cruise ship heading from your country to Egypt and work aboard it. If you want to learn about real estate then get a job in a real estate office and get paid for it. If you love travelling then go and get paid to be a flight attendant or pilot. You will get really cheap airfares and see half the world!

Try and get some experience for your time and outlay. I get

to help a lot of people with their wealth building, but I get a buzz out of it and get paid as well. The money is just the by-product of the success. By following your heart and doing what you love you will achieve more, faster.

You may say to yourself, *"I don't know what I want to do!"* Go and try something completely different. Just keep interacting with people everywhere you go. You will come across someone or something that presents a great opportunity for you.

The saying, *"It's not what you know, but who you know,"* has got me a long way in life. I find that if I show high energy levels and be a leader of 'me' others are attracted to that and opportunities come to me, plus the people who I attract are high quality people with similar values.

I now associate with world champions in sport and millionaires in money, and life coaches with outstanding results to their name, and it has made a huge difference to me. But only you can choose to make a difference in your life.

Follow the chapters if that is easiest for you. Start with 'choice' and make the choice to do something different, and then accept responsibility and don't defer responsibility any longer.

Stop making excuses and start to make a difference. Understand that sacrifice and discipline starts in the mind and is put in place first mentally, and then by taking physical action.

Manage your time to fit it all in. Be ruthless with time and gracious with people. Time is your most important asset along with your health, so treat it carefully. But remember to allocate a portion of time and energy to your wealth.

80% of what I do related to making money appears boring. I do however, get a buzz out of what money can provide.

I also enjoy seeing others achieve financial success, take their money and achieve what they want to as well. I focus on my investing daily and I am always trying to improve it in any area possible. I do find that my bank account is a reflection of all the other things I do in life. When I stop exercising or donating to charity I seem to have less energy, and because I stop giving less money seems to come back to me.

Start by putting into practice a few new things you have learned. Buy as many personal development books and tapes as you can, attend seminars often and invest money into yourself and your personal development. Others will try and hold you back from doing this and other self-improvement action steps, but when you pass them by in your new Ferrari, they will soon wonder what is happening.

Some do, some don't, so what! What other people think of you is none of your business! While you make it happen, others watch it happen and some people wonder what actually did happen! The more you want something and the more successful you become the more others will try and hold you back.

Go hard at it and never quit. This is life and you can't quit, it's real and it's on! Play ball because the siren has started. You're dead a long time so ask yourself, *"Is it going to matter in one hundred years time?"* Maybe not, but can you leave a trail or make a difference to someone else's life?

Only change what isn't working and continue to follow through to the end. Too many people quit in life before the final payout. If they had just hung in there for a bit longer they would realise the cash is coming soon. But they seem to quit just before the day the money is due.

Don't mistake hanging in there for riding a loser. If you're flogging a dead horse, it isn't going to get up and run, so identify quickly if it's worth your time and decide whether to move on or stay and keep working. Judge your time by the income or result the project at hand will produce for you.

Remember, association and whom you hang around makes a big difference, so change your environment if need be. Negative people have negative energy, so avoid control freaks and be careful of manipulation.

You can do it. But only you can do it for yourself! Nobody else cares enough to do it for you. There are a lot of 'nice' people out there, but remember, nice stands for 'Nothing Inside Cares Enough' and as far as I'm concerned you owe it to yourself to care for your body and mind.

If you were given one car at the age of 18 and that car had to last you the rest of life, then you would probably look after it well. You would wash it and service it regularly. You wouldn't thrash it and you wouldn't let someone else drive it. So why are so many people abusing their bodies and lives? You only get one shot at life and if you crash it hard enough it's a write off. So don't hand the keys of your life over to someone else, as they will more than likely slam it into a tree. Look after it as you only have one. Put good fuel into it and get it serviced often. Massage and exercise is a good service and so is a bit of loving or a work out in the gym.

Keep in mind, all you need is the street name that is your goal, and a street directory that will tell you how to get there. You may make a few wrong turns along the way, but as soon as you realise that you're off the track, just pull over and re-check your map. Don't speed and stick to the rules.

But develop your own rules, as well as sticking to the compulsory ones along the way. If you get a flat tyre, get out and change it. It might be raining, but you can turn on the heaters and you will soon dry. When you get there you can hop out and say: *"Ah, I made it, and it feels good!"* Sure your legs may be a bit stiff, but they will soon recover.

So hop to it and work out your destination. This is just a dream with a date on it. Your map to get there is going to be your education, and your knowledge will allow you to plan out your journey. If real estate is going to be your financial vehicle then you had better get busy studying that. If the share market is going to be your choice then go and follow through on it. If sport is your passion then you had better start training. If you want something badly enough you will get it.

So do it now and take physical action, almost everyone else is sleeping, so you have no competition except yourself!

There is no such thing as scarcity. There is an abundance of whatever you need, love, money or time. There is tons of it so go and claim your portion!

I know you deserve it and you know you do too, so put in the effort. I still think you could sum it all up into one sentence and Nike got it right. Don't just talk about it, **just do it**. Keep in mind that 'success is not convenient but the rewards are.' Just do the important things while you can and not when you have to.

Chapter 13

Closing

This book is more about what you need to do to yourself than a 'how to' book on investing. I have chosen this as the content to share with you because of my experience. I found that focusing on me was the key to achieving financially.

A lot of people have contributed to my life in various ways and I recommend finding good people in your life to hang around and to learn from. Watch out for rip-off people and scams, and be careful of free advice, as it can often be the most expensive.

In my experience, I have found that you cannot learn everything by asking questions and there comes a point if you want to progress, you have to **just do it**! You will learn by your mistakes, you will grow and progress faster by accepting mistakes as lessons and moving on from that. If you need to change tack then do it. You cannot control the wind, but you can adjust the sails to embrace change and accept that change will have to take place at certain times.

Self-motivation is only difficult because you have not asked yourself what the alternative is going to be. It is easy to get caught up in the modern day lifestyle, but it really is not what I consider a lifestyle. I have chosen to not accept less than I deserve and I am prepared to do what it takes to get my self-satisfaction. Then I move onto the next challenge and away I go again.

There is a lot to do in life rather than working to pay off your house and end up stuck in the one suburb of the one city of the one country for the rest of life! No thanks, not me. You need a base for sure and somewhere to call home, but I want the freedom of choice and I will report only to one person, myself. I choose when I wake up and if I feel like working hard then so be it. If I love it then I will work hard.

Cash is the easy bit. Money is a measure of what you were prepared to give up to get it. It is far from the most important thing in life, but it can supply you with the ability to do and achieve all the important things in life. 'Balanced' people don't get too far in life and if you are going to consume time doing something then you might as well give it your best shot anyway.

You came to this world with nothing and you will leave with nothing. It's only what you do in between that counts, and the difference you can make to other people's lives along the way.

If you're not sure where to start, do what I did when I was very young and join a strong networking marketing company with quality products. There are two reasons I recommend this – firstly, because this strategy was what first got me exposed to personal development material. Secondly, because you can create a business and an income for yourself – and you're going to need cash flow!

The other huge advantage is the association with the other members and business builders. They have positive outlooks on life and are results-oriented, plus they do not sell their time to generate income either! They need to ensure your success so they can succeed and that is the best part of it. You get paid to help others achieve.

I cannot recommend joining one enough, and to this day getting involved with network marketing was the reason I got somewhere financially and personally. Even just for the personal development, I suggest you try joining a good one and stick it out. Don't even begin to listen to what the critics have to say about network marketing. They are just living below the line.

Consume less, drink more water, exercise a bit more, sleep less and eat more fruit and vegetables. Take short holidays regularly, avoid consumer credit, leverage your time, stick to your word and if you say you are going to do something, do it.

Do something for someone else less fortunate than you. Make sure you always work harder on yourself than you do on your job, and give lots of love to everyone around you.

Don't go to your death bed wishing you had spent more time with loved ones or wishing you told someone something you didn't. Go visit them right now and hug them. Keep on smiling and when times get tough accept it as a test and pick yourself up and go again. No one will do it for you so get used to helping yourself. You can only help someone who is prepared to help themselves.

So go for it and claim your share of life. You do deserve it and you can do it.

Don't wish that life was easier, wish that you were better. Hug someone and tell them you love them. Have a laugh often and smile at someone as they pass you in the street. The easiest way to get a smile is to give one.

Take a bit of a chance and try something new. When everyone else zigs, you have to zag. Take up a sport you have not done before and put a bit of spring in your stride. It's only what you make of it and you only get one shot at it. Live above the line and be grateful always. Donate to a charity and most importantly donate to yourself. Make mankind your customer and let God be your boss. If **'you need a rocket'** then the best person to give it to you is yourself.

Do something special with your life and answer to yourself. You can choose to fail or you can choose to succeed, but either way it's your choice.

Thank you.

Martin Ayles.

About The Author

Martin Ayles was born and raised in Adelaide, South Australia. Although not Business Smart in his early days, he has since gone on to prove himself time over as a well established and proven property developer working outside the realms of convention to generate well deserved results.

In 2002 he wrote " You Need a Rocket" and this was the beginning of a lucrative passion project that accidently allowed him to also showcase himself as a brilliant public speaker. Through the lessons learnt in Business and the Building trade, he established himself as a great teacher both from the stage and one on one. He has continued to educate thousands of people over the years leaving a profound message every time combined with useful and practical information.

When Marty is not teaching others or developing his own portfolio you will catch him on a river somewhere water-skiing. He is an accomplished piano player and continually donates to his time and resources to various charities that he is passionate about.

www.martinayles.com
Email: info@martinayles.com

Publishing through a successful Australian publisher. Brolga provides:

- Editorial appraisal
- Cover design
- Typesetting
- Printing
- Author promotion
    - National book trade distribution, including sales, marketing and distribution through Macmillan Australia.
    - International book trade distribution
    - Worldwide e-Book distribution

For details and inquiries, contact:
Brolga Publishing Pty Ltd
PO Box 12544
A'Beckett St VIC 8006

Phone: 0414 608 494
admin@brolgapublishing.com.au
markzocchi@brolgapublishing.com.au
ABN: 46 063 962 443